Landform Top Tens

The World's Most Amazing Deserts

Anna Claybourne

Raintree

Chicago, Illinois

www.heinemannraintree.com
Visit our website to find out more information about Heinemann-Raintree books.

To order:
☎ Phone 888-454-2279
💻 Visit www.heinemannraintree.com to browse our catalog and order online.

Edited by Louise Galpine, Kate DeVilliers, and Rachel Howells
Designed by Victoria Bevan and Geoff Ward
Original illustrations © Capstone Global Library Limited
Illustrated by Geoff Ward
Picture research by Hannah Taylor
Production by Alison Parsons

Printed and bound in China by CTPS

13 12 11 10 09
10 9 8 7 6 5 4 3 2 1

Library of Congress Cataloging-in-Publication Data

Claybourne, Anna.
  The world's most amazing deserts / Anna Claybourne.
     p. cm. -- (Landform top tens)
  Includes bibliographical references and index.
  ISBN 978-1-4109-3701-8 (hc) -- ISBN 978-1-4109-3709-4 (pb)
  1. Deserts--Juvenile literature. I. Title.
  GB612.C54 2008
  551.41'5--dc22
                              2008051495

Acknowledgments

We would like to thank the following for permission to reproduce photographs: Ardea.com pp. **6** (Alan Greensmith), **8** and **11** (M. Watson), **9** (Bob Gibbons), **16** (Chris Harvey), **26** (Chris Knights); Corbis pp. **13** (Lanz Von Horsten; Gallo Images), **14–15** (Blaine Harrington III); FLPA pp. **7** and **21** (Imagebroker/ Stefan Auth), **12** (Minden Pictures/ Michael & Patricia Fogden), **20** (Minden Pictures/ Cyril Ruoso), **25** (Roger Tidman), **27** (Chris and Tilde Stuart/Holt); naturepl pp. **10** (HUW CORDEY), **17** (Laurent Geslin); Photolibrary pp. **4–5** (Corbis), **18** (Hemis/ Bertrand Gardel), **19** (Robert Harding Travel/ Christina Gascoigne), **22** (Milton Wordley), **23** (Ted Mead), **24** (Robert Harding Travel/ Geoff Renner).

Background images by Getty Images (Photodisc) and Photolibrary (Brand X Pictures).

Cover photograph of sand dunes in the Namib Desert, reproduced with permission of Corbis (Michele Westmorland).

We would like to thank Nick Lapthorn for his invaluable help in the preparation of this book.

Every effort has been made to contact copyright holders of material reproduced in this book. Any omissions will be rectified in subsequent printings if notice is given to the publishers.

Disclaimer

All the Internet addresses (URLs) given in this book were valid at the time of going to press. However, due to the dynamic nature of the Internet, some addresses may have changed, or sites may have changed or ceased to exist since publication. While the author and publishers regret any inconvenience this may cause readers, no responsibility for any such changes can be accepted by either the author or the publishers. It is recommended that adults supervise children on the Internet.

Contents

Some words are printed in bold, **like this.** You can find out what they mean by looking in the glossary on page 31.

Deserts

A desert is a place that is very dry. There is not much rain, and hardly any streams, rivers, or lakes. With so little water, it can be hard for plants and animals to survive. The word "desert" means "deserted" or "empty."

However, most deserts are not totally empty. Some creatures do live there. They have **adapted** to be able to live without much water. Some deserts even have towns and cities.

Every type of desert

Not all deserts are sandy and hot. There are rocky or pebbly deserts, **scrub** deserts with low bushes and trees, and even snowy and icy deserts! Even the hottest deserts are often very cold at night.

How dry is a desert?

It is hard to say exactly how dry a place has to be to be called a desert. One way to decide is to measure the **rainfall**. Most experts agree that a true desert has less than 25 cm (10 in.) of rain per year.

Saguaro cactuses, a type of desert plant, grow in the Sonoran Desert in Mexico.

The Sahara Desert

The Sahara is the world's biggest and hottest desert. It stretches across North Africa, covering an area almost the size of Canada. The hottest temperature ever recorded on Earth was measured in the Sahara, at El Azizia, Libya. It was 58°C (136°F).

Water in the desert

An **oasis** is a natural spring in a desert. Oases form where underground water comes to Earth's surface.

These trees and shrubs are growing around an oasis in part of the Sahara Desert.

SAHARA DESERT

LOCATION:
NORTH AFRICA, INCLUDING ALGERIA, CHAD, EGYPT, LIBYA, MALI, MAURITANIA, MOROCCO, NIGER, WESTERN SAHARA, SUDAN, AND TUNISIA

TYPE OF DESERT:
HOT, SANDY, AND ROCKY

AREA:
9,100,000 KM² (3,500,000 SQ MILES)

AVERAGE RAINFALL:
127 MM (5 IN.) PER YEAR

THAT'S AMAZING!
FOSSILS OF CROCODILES AND OTHER WATER ANIMALS SHOW THAT THE SAHARA WAS ONCE A SOGGY SWAMP.

Sahara Desert

AFRICA

Atlantic Ocean

Indian Ocean

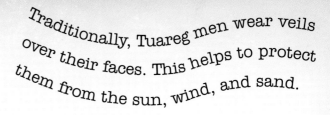

Traditionally, Tuareg men wear veils over their faces. This helps to protect them from the sun, wind, and sand.

Who lives there?

The Sahara is home to animals such as snakes and lizards, scorpions, and the addax, a rare type of antelope. There are people, too, including groups such as the Tuareg. They are **nomads,** moving from place to place. They lead their herds of camels, sheep, and goats around to find water, and they camp in tents along the way.

The Mojave Desert

The Mojave Desert in North America is home to scorching Death Valley, the lowest, hottest, and driest place in the United States. In Death Valley, the temperature can be over 54°C (130°F) in summer. But in winter, parts of the Mojave are below freezing! The Mojave Desert is tiny compared to some deserts, but it is full of extremes and fascinating sights.

Death Valley is a long, deep valley surrounded by high mountains. The mountains trap the sun's heat, making the valley extremely hot.

Joshua trees

The Mojave is famous for its Joshua trees. Their thick, spiky leaves are good at storing water. This tree has developed a way of collecting as much rain as it can. Its leaves gather rainwater and make it flow down to the base of the tree, watering the ground below it.

MOJAVE DESERT

LOCATION:
CALIFORNIA, NEVADA, ARIZONA, AND UTAH, NORTH AMERICA

TYPE OF DESERT:
HOT, SANDY, MOUNTAINOUS, AND **SCRUBBY**

AREA:
65,000 KM² (25,000 SQ MILES)

AVERAGE RAINFALL:
130 MM (5 IN.) PER YEAR

THAT'S AMAZING!
THE LOWEST PART OF DEATH VALLEY IS 86 METERS (282 FEET) BELOW **SEA LEVEL**.

NORTH AMERICA

Mojave Desert

Pacific Ocean

Atlantic Ocean

Joshua trees are easy to spot, with their bunches of leaves and crooked shape.

The Gobi Desert

GOBI DESERT

LOCATION:
CHINA AND MONGOLIA, ASIA

TYPE OF DESERT:
PEBBLY, **SCRUBBY**, SANDY, ROCKY, AND COLD

AREA:
1,295,000 KM² (500,000 SQ MILES)

AVERAGE RAINFALL:
180 MM (7 IN.) PER YEAR

THAT'S AMAZING!
TEMPERATURES IN THE GOBI CAN RANGE FROM -40°C (-40°F) TO OVER 50°C (122°F).

The Gobi is the biggest desert in Asia and the fourth biggest desert in the world. It is also one of the world's coldest deserts. It is often icy and snowy, although it can be very hot in summer.

Patches of snow lie among the **sand dunes** in parts of the Gobi Desert in Mongolia.

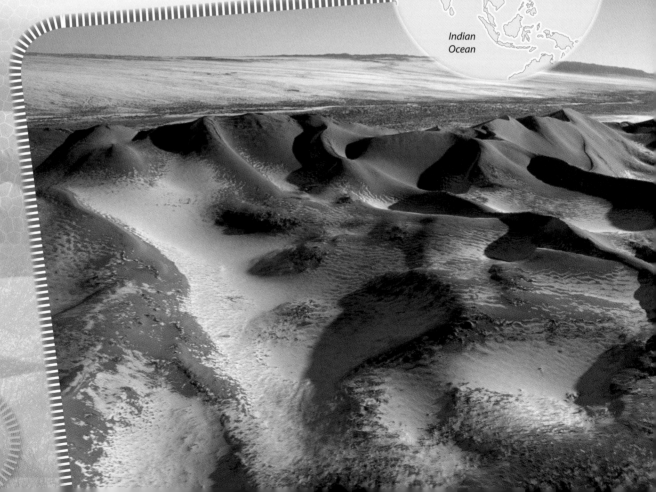

ASIA

Gobi Desert

Pacific Ocean

Indian Ocean

Bactrian camels

Bactrian camels are camels with two humps. There are lots of **domesticated** Bactrians, but fewer than 1,000 wild ones. These wild camels live in the Gobi Desert. They are very shy and hard to find.

In the rain shadow

The Gobi lies in two countries: Mongolia and China. It is a **rain shadow** desert. Rain shadow deserts are created when clouds blow toward mountains. As they are forced up the mountain slopes, the clouds get colder and fall as rain. On the other side of the mountains, there are no clouds left, so a desert forms.

The Namib Desert

The Namib Desert in southwest Africa is one of the world's oldest deserts. Scientists think it may have existed for 80 million years. The Namib is a **coastal** desert, meaning it is next to the sea. This is unusual. Most deserts are far from the sea or are separated from it by mountains.

Weird wildlife

Some strange creatures live in the Namib. The shovel-snouted lizard does a "thermal dance," lifting its feet off the hot sand two at a time to let them cool down. The weird weltwitschia plant has only two wide, twisted leaves and can live for over 1,000 years.

A web-footed gecko in the Namib licks its eyes with its tongue to clean away sand and dust.

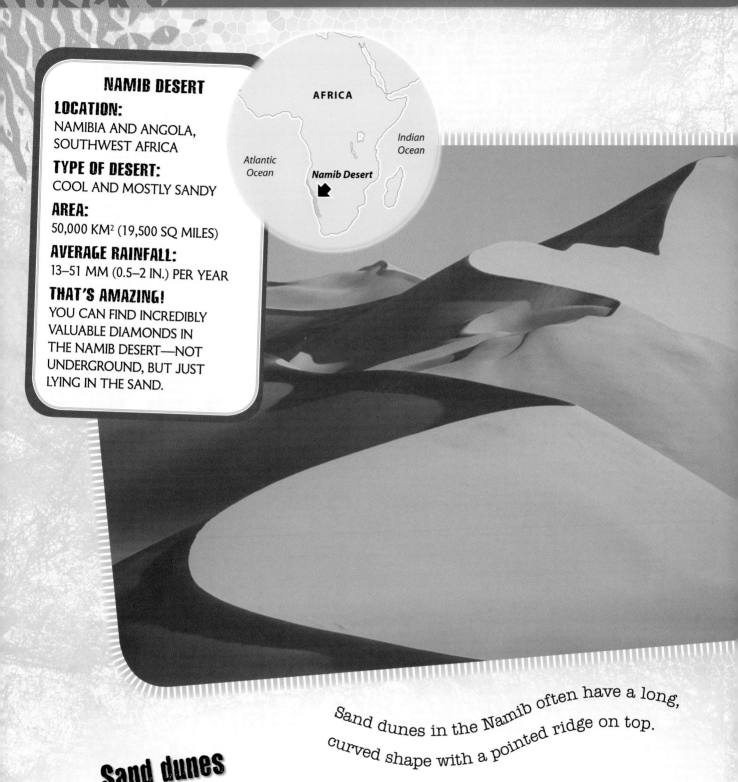

NAMIB DESERT

LOCATION:
NAMIBIA AND ANGOLA,
SOUTHWEST AFRICA

TYPE OF DESERT:
COOL AND MOSTLY SANDY

AREA:
50,000 KM² (19,500 SQ MILES)

AVERAGE RAINFALL:
13–51 MM (0.5–2 IN.) PER YEAR

THAT'S AMAZING!
YOU CAN FIND INCREDIBLY
VALUABLE DIAMONDS IN
THE NAMIB DESERT—NOT
UNDERGROUND, BUT JUST
LYING IN THE SAND.

AFRICA

Indian
Ocean

Atlantic
Ocean

Namib Desert

Sand dunes in the Namib often have a long,
curved shape with a pointed ridge on top.

Sand dunes

Sand dunes are heaps of sand. They form when the wind
blows across a desert, making the sand pile up. Much of
the Namib Desert is an **erg** or **dune sea**—a big area of
sandy dunes, with hardly any plants.

The Atacama Desert

The mountainous Atacama Desert in Chile is one of the driest deserts in the world. There are some parts of it that have not been rained on since records began. Because it is such a dry place, not many **species** of plants and animals live there.

The Atacama Desert has hardly any rain, but more than one million people live there.

ATACAMA DESERT

LOCATION:
CHILE, SOUTH AMERICA

TYPE OF DESERT:
COOL, SANDY, AND ROCKY

AREA:
103,000 KM²
(40,000 SQ MILES)

AVERAGE RAINFALL:
AROUND 10 MM (0.4 IN.)
PER YEAR

THAT'S AMAZING!
THE DRIEST TOWN IN THE WORLD IS QUILLAGUA, IN THE ATACAMA. IN AN AVERAGE YEAR IT GETS LESS THAN 0.5 MM (0.02 IN.) OF RAIN!

Pacific Ocean

SOUTH AMERICA

Atlantic Ocean

Atacama Desert

Double rain shadow

The Atacama is a **rain shadow** desert. It is surrounded by mountains. On one side, Chile's **coastal** mountains block clouds coming from the Pacific Ocean. On the west, the Andes mountain range blocks clouds that form over the Amazon rain forest.

Ancient mummies

Amazing **mummies** up to 7,000 years old have been discovered in the Atacama. They are the remains of the Chinchorro people, who stuffed and painted dead bodies to preserve them.

The Kalahari Desert

Africa's Kalahari Desert is probably more full of life than any other desert. It is famous for its rich wildlife, including lions, antelopes, wild dogs, ants, lizards, and acacia trees. Although it is called a desert, the Kalahari is actually a **semi-desert**—an area that is dry, but not a true desert.

The Okavango

The Okavango River flows into part of the Kalahari Desert and floods an area every year. Waterbirds, wildebeest, elephants, hippos, and crocodiles live there, as well as trees, reeds, and beautiful water lilies.

A tourist travels by boat through the Okavango Delta to spot wildlife.

KALAHARI DESERT

LOCATION:
BOTSWANA, NAMIBIA, AND SOUTH AFRICA, AFRICA

TYPE OF DESERT:
HOT, SANDY, SHRUBBY, AND GRASSY

AREA:
650,000 KM² (250,000 SQ MILES)

AVERAGE RAINFALL:
250–400 MM (10–16 IN.) PER YEAR

THAT'S AMAZING!
THE NAME "KALAHARI" COMES FROM A LOCAL WORD MEANING "GREAT THIRST."

AFRICA

Indian Ocean

Atlantic Ocean

Kalahari Desert

San hunter-gatherers use small bows and arrows for hunting food in the desert.

Meet the San

The San people of the Kalahari have lived as **hunter-gatherers** for thousands of years. Instead of farming, they hunt animals and collect nuts, eggs, fruit, and berries.

The Dead Sea Desert

The Dead Sea, in Israel, is very much like a desert—but it is a huge lake! It has hardly any wildlife, however, because it is so salty that fish and other animals and plants cannot live in it. Only a few **bacteria** can survive.

The huge amount of salt dissolved in the Dead Sea means that people float very high in the water.

DEAD SEA DESERT

LOCATION:
ISRAEL AND JORDAN, ASIA

TYPE OF DESERT:
HOT, ROCKY DESERT
SURROUNDING A SALT LAKE

AREA:
1,010 KM² (390 SQ MILES)

AVERAGE RAINFALL:
AROUND 100 MM (4 IN.) PER YEAR

THAT'S AMAZING!
WATER IN THE DEAD SEA IS
OVER EIGHT TIMES SALTIER
THAN NORMAL SEAWATER.

ASIA

AFRICA

Dead Sea Desert

As water evaporates from the Dead Sea, it leaves these crusty white salt deposits behind.

Desert shore

The Dead Sea lies in a real desert, too. It is surrounded by a very low, dry, hot desert landscape. There is very little rain. Instead, rivers flow into the Dead Sea, and the heat makes their water **evaporate**. Over time, all the salt in the water gets left behind, and the Dead Sea gets saltier and saltier.

The Thar Desert

The Thar Desert in India is the world's most heavily **populated** desert. It has towns and cities, as well as farmers who herd animals or harvest desert trees for wood. Tourists often go there, too, to see the desert's beautiful stone castles and palaces and to enjoy its festivals. Since it is not as dry as some deserts, it has plenty of plants and animals.

These Hanuman langurs, a type of monkey, are sitting on a rock in the Thar Desert.

Water from underground

In the past, most people in the Thar Desert got their water from ponds that filled up whenever it rained, and from springs. But the desert's big cities, such as Jaipur, now also pump up water from deep underground.

THAR DESERT

LOCATION:
INDIA AND A SMALL PART OF PAKISTAN, ASIA

TYPE OF DESERT:
HOT, SANDY, **SCRUBBY**, PEBBLY, AND HILLY

AREA:
200,000 KM² (77,000 SQ MILES)

AVERAGE RAINFALL:
AROUND 250 MM (10 IN.) PER YEAR

THAT'S AMAZING!
MORE THAN 12 MILLION PEOPLE LIVE IN THE THAR DESERT.

ASIA

Thar Desert

Pacific Ocean

Indian Ocean

Thar people enjoy holding competitions. This camel is entering a camel beauty contest!

The Simpson Desert

The Simpson Desert in the middle of Australia is an **erg** with the longest **sand dunes** in the world. Some are 200 km (125 miles) long. It would take two hours to drive from one end of a dune this big to the other.

The Simpson Desert's massive dunes make it difficult to cross in a vehicle.

SIMPSON DESERT

LOCATION:
AUSTRALIA, **AUSTRALASIA**

TYPE OF DESERT:
HOT, SANDY, **SCRUBBY**, AND ROCKY

AREA:
143,000 KM² (55,000 SQ MILES)

AVERAGE RAINFALL:
200 MM (8 IN.) PER YEAR

THAT'S AMAZING!
ONE SIMPSON DESERT FLOWER IS CALLED THE POACHED EGG DAISY, BECAUSE IT LOOKS JUST LIKE A POACHED EGG!

AUSTRALASIA

Pacific Ocean

Indian Ocean

Simpson Desert

AUSTRALIA

A kowari leaves its burrow to hunt for insects and spiders to eat.

Unique animals

Australia has wildlife that is not found anywhere else in the world. In the Simpson Desert, you can find trees, grasses, flowers, lizards, birds such as the gray grasswren, and **marsupials.** Marsupials, such as kangaroos, are Australian animals that carry their babies in a pouch. Simpson Desert marsupials include the kowari, a rat-like animal with a bushy tail, which lives in burrows in the sand.

Antarctica

The Sahara is the biggest true desert in the world. But some experts say that Antarctica, the **continent** around the South Pole, should also be counted as a desert. If it is counted, it is the biggest desert of all.

People can live in Antarctica, but only because they take in food supplies and fuel for keeping warm.

ANTARCTICA

LOCATION:
ANTARCTICA

TYPE OF DESERT:
COLD, ICY, AND ROCKY

AREA:
14,000,000 KM² (5,400,000 SQ MILES)

AVERAGE RAINFALL:
50–200 MM (2–8 IN.), BUT IT MAINLY FALLS AS SNOW

THAT'S AMAZING!
THE COLDEST TEMPERATURE EVER RECORDED ON EARTH WAS MEASURED IN VOSTOK, ANTARCTICA. IT WAS -89.4°C (-129°F).

ANTARCTICA

Southern Ocean

Emperor penguins hunt for fish in the sea, but go inland to lay eggs and care for their chicks.

Watery wastes

Antarctica is not short of water—it is covered in it. But a lot of the continent is very dry because almost all the water is frozen into solid ice. Plants and animals cannot drink water when it is frozen. Because of this, there is very little wildlife in Antarctica, except in the sea around its coasts.

Inland (away from the sea), there are only a few living things. They include penguins, which spend some of the time in the sea, as well as insects and spiders, mosses, and **lichens**.

Deserts in Danger

Deserts are important homes for plants, animals, and millions of people. But desert **ecosystems**—communities of living things—are very delicate. Because there is little water, even a slight change can make the difference between surviving and not surviving.

Crops such as these sugar beets can wilt and die when the climate becomes too dry.

Changing deserts

Deserts naturally grow and shrink over time, as the world's **climate** changes. **Global warming** is now making some deserts hotter and drier, and this is making them expand (get bigger). This is called **desertification**. The Gobi Desert, for example, is expanding by over 3,000 km² (1,150 sq miles) every year.

A backhoe makes holes ready for tree planting on a desert island in Arabia.

Helping deserts

One way to stop deserts from getting too dry is to plant desert grasses and shrubs in the sand. They keep the sand together and help it to hold water. This gradually turns desert back into **semi-desert**. Some desert cities, such as Jaipur in the Thar Desert, are building pipelines to carry water in from faraway rivers. This helps people avoid using up too much of the desert's scarce water.

Desert Facts and Figures

Deserts can be swelteringly hot or icy cold. They can be covered in huge **sand dunes** or filled with rock formations. Some are so dry that hardly anything lives there, while others have towns and cities. Which desert do you think is the most amazing?

This map of the world shows all the deserts described in this book.

Arctic Ocean

NORTH AMERICA

Mojave Desert

Atlantic Ocean

EUROPE

ASIA

Gobi Desert

Dead Sea Desert

Thar Desert

Sahara Desert

AFRICA

Pacific Ocean

Pacific Ocean

SOUTH AMERICA

Atacama Desert

Namib Desert

Kalahari Desert

Indian Ocean

AUSTRALASIA

Simpson Desert

Southern Ocean

ANTARCTICA

SAHARA DESERT
TYPE OF DESERT:
HOT, SANDY, AND ROCKY

AREA:
9,100,000 KM^2
(3,500,000 SQ MILES)

MOJAVE DESERT
TYPE OF DESERT:
HOT, SANDY, MOUNTAINOUS, AND **SCRUBBY**

AREA:
65,000 KM^2
(25,000 SQ MILES)

GOBI DESERT
TYPE OF DESERT:
PEBBLY, SCRUBBY, SANDY, ROCKY, AND COLD

AREA:
1,295,000 KM^2
(500,000 SQ MILES)

NAMIB DESERT
TYPE OF DESERT:
COOL AND MOSTLY SANDY

AREA:
50,000 KM^2
(19,500 SQ MILES)

ATACAMA DESERT
TYPE OF DESERT:
COOL, SANDY, AND ROCKY

AREA:
103,000 KM^2
(40,000 SQ MILES)

KALAHARI DESERT
TYPE OF DESERT:
HOT, SANDY, SHRUBBY, AND GRASSY

AREA:
650,000 KM^2
(250,000 SQ MILES)

DEAD SEA DESERT
TYPE OF DESERT:
HOT, ROCKY DESERT SURROUNDING A SALT LAKE

AREA:
1,010 KM^2
(390 SQ MILES)

THAR DESERT
TYPE OF DESERT:
HOT, SANDY, SCRUBBY, PEBBLY, AND HILLY

AREA:
200,000 KM^2
(77,000 SQ MILES)

SIMPSON DESERT
TYPE OF DESERT:
HOT, SANDY, **SCRUBBY**, AND ROCKY

AREA:
143,000 KM^2
(55,000 SQ MILES)

ANTARCTICA
TYPE OF DESERT:
COLD, ICY, AND ROCKY

AREA:
14,000,000 KM^2
(5,400,000 SQ MILES)

Find Out More

Books to read

Chambers, Catherine, and Nicholas Lapthorn. *Mapping Earthforms: Deserts*. Chicago: Heinemann Library, 2008.

Ganeri, Anita. *Horrible Geography: Desperate Deserts*. New York: Scholastic, 2008.

Green, Jen. *Geography Now!: Deserts and Polar Regions Around the World*. New York: PowerKids, 2009.

Websites

Desert Field Trip
www.field-trips.org/sci/desert
This web page features an online desert "tour" that includes fascinating facts about many of the world's deserts.

Enchanted Learning Desert Printouts
www.enchantedlearning.com/biomes/desert/desert
Find facts, pictures, and printouts on wildlife in different deserts around the world on this web page.

The National Park Service: Mojave National Preserve
www.nps.gov/archive/moja/home.htm
Learn more about the Mojave Desert, including the kinds of plants and animals found there, on this website.

U.S. Geological Survey: Deserts
http://pubs.usgs.gov/gip/deserts/contents
Find very detailed facts, figures, and photographs about all aspects of deserts on this website.

Glossary

adapt change over time to suit the surroundings

Australasia term used to describe Australia, New Zealand, and a series of nearby islands in the Pacific Ocean

bacteria tiny living things that can only be seen through a microscope

climate overall weather patterns on Earth, or in a part of the world

coastal alongside or on the coast

continent continuous landmass. There are seven continents on Earth.

desertification turning from normal land or semi-desert into a true desert

domesticated animals bred to be kept by humans

dune sea another name for an erg

ecosystem community of living things and the place they live in

erg area of desert made up of sand dunes

evaporate change from a liquid into a gas

global warming gradual warming of Earth caused by pollution

hunter-gatherer someone who collects and hunts for food

lichen type of living thing made up of tiny plants and fungi that form a mat on a rocky surface

marsupial animal that carries its babies in a pouch on its front

mummy dead body that has been preserved by wrapping it in bandages

nomad someone who has no fixed home but moves around

oasis natural spring in a desert that provides fresh water

populated filled with people

rainfall amount of rain that a place receives

rain shadow type of desert that forms when mountains stop rainclouds from reaching an area of land

sand dune heap of sand that forms when wind blows across a desert

scrub type of desert landscape with some desert plants, low trees, and bushes

sea level level, or height, of the surface of the sea

semi-desert area that is dry, but not dry enough to be counted as a true desert

species particular type of living thing

Index